In Company

Lines of Work

Kate Bernadette Benedict

Kate BB

CW Books

Published by CW Books
P.O. Box 541106
Cincinnati, OH 45254-1106

ISBN: 9781936370580
LCCN: 2011945150

Poetry Editor: Kevin Walzer
Business Editor: Lori Jareo

Visit us on the web at www.readcwbooks.com

Acknowledgments

The author thanks the editors of the following journals where some of the poems in this volume first appeared:

Across the Board, Bent Pin Quarterly, BigCityLit, Fringe, The Ghazal Page, Gin Bender, Mannequin Envy, The New Plains Review, Pig Iron, Poetry Magazine, Poets On, The Red River Review, Snakeskin, Soundzine, Thema, Without Halos.

******

Thanks also to the editors of the following anthologies:

"View from the Front Desk" and "In Company" appear in *The Literature of Work*, eds. Sheila E. Murphy, John G. Sperling and John D. Murphy, University of Phoenix Press (Phoenix, AZ), 1991.

"Sanctuary" and "Resignation" appear in *Paperwork*, ed. Tom Wayman, Harbour Publishing Co., Ltd. (Madeira Park, BC), 1991.

"Off Duty" appears in *If I Had a Hammer: Women's Work*, ed. Sandra Martz, Papier Maché Press (Watsonville, California), 1989.

******

The author also thanks her many bosses for tolerating an employee who was occasionally disgruntled and chronically distracted, and gives a special nod to Jim, Jack, Beverly, Nan, Alice, Ravi, Ruvan, Gene, Greg, and Denis. She was devoted to them, in her fashion.

Table of Contents

1. Quotidian Soliloquies
View from the Front Desk....................11
The Stenographer Muses....................12
The Sorceress....................13
Occupational Hazards....................15
Words for a Temp....................17
Words for a Latter-Day Luddite....................19
Sanctuary....................21
I Hear America Complaining....................22
My Demon Lover....................23
Green Man....................25
The Beauty in the Bun....................26
Memorandum....................27
Wail from the 29th Floor....................28
Crying for Girls....................29
Resignation....................30

2. Practical Lies
Universe Management....................35
The Manager of Change....................37
An Office Bestiary....................39
The Misbegotten Detention of the Unkempt....................41
Presence of the Absence....................43
Practical Lies....................44
Morning in Sodom....................45
Travailelle....................46

3. Love and Work
Getting It Done....................49
After Long Days Visiting the Nursing
  Home, I Return to the Office 50
The Blood Drive....................51
Waiting for Elevation....................53
Women Dancing With Women....................55
Dead Matter....................57
Corporate Retreat....................59
Off Duty....................61
Torpid Transit....................63

Invitation to a Baby Shower in the
    Corporate Law Library..64
Fifth Avenue Gothic..65
The Triumph of Eros...67
A Roadblock in the Negotiations..................................68
Quotidian Ballad...69
High Floor Ballad..70
Love and Work..71

4. After

Canticle from a Cubicle..75
Let Go...76
After..77
The Unemployment Office...78
In Company..80

Coda

The Transformation...83

1. Quotidian Soliloquies

View from the Front Desk

I'm in before anyone. I'm a sterling employee.
I'm here when the first hiss of air whooshes
from the vents, sibilant as a librarian's shushes.
Then the phones ring, the bosses come, the raree

begins. I take it all in. Whatever messengers bring—
parcels, lunches, roses—I accept.
If all three come at once, I'm quite adept.
There's room on my desk for everything.

It's the lulls that throw me: minutes that drag
on and on and on and no bells ring. Workers from inside
whizz past, flushing with purpose and pride.
I drum my lacquered nails or claw my bag

for gum. Then all bells blow at once! I grieve
no more: my lot's to wait, my calling to receive.

The Stenographer Muses

My dictator! You speak and I surrender,
I love. I tuck my freedom away like a glove.

I'm a dead page your words enliven,
a vessel they possess.
Though unsubstantial, they take hold of me,
their chosen medium.

They employ me, ear to fingertip,
and I allow this, sacrificially.

I live to give, I live to be of use.

Once inside, my fluids change them marvelously.
See how they stream from my pen in cryptic glyphs!

I could be Sybil, sitting here,
cloaking the sun god's wisdom
with my quirky script,
or the keeper of some awful gnosis.

Yes, the company fears me and pays me well.
O my dictator, tell, tell.

The Sorceress

That's me, all right,
duplicating, replicating,
turning one page into ten,
ten into ten thousand,
then lifting each white bundle
out and up, out and up
as more come out and up—
like rabbits from a hat!

It's workday hokum
under fluorescent lights—
my follow spots—
and the din,
the steady clapping of the great devices,
that, that
is my applause.

I'm very good at what I do!
Give me a ream of bond
and with a finger flick
I'll fill each page
with graphic marvels.
Give me yellow sheets, and blue,
and with sleight of hand
I'll turn them into rainbow collations,
transmuted, three-holed,
piled in perfect rows.
Come, flutter their edges—
it's a boffo trick,
a good old-fashioned wonder
like the bird from the babushka
or the levitating man.

How I blaze with the static the platen radiates!
My long hair's frizzed,
my handshake snaps with light.

Yes, I am this office's sorceress,
efficient and radiant witch—
yet you hardly notice me,
you grab your stacks and go.
Ladies, gentlemen,
can't you see what I can do?
One day O one day soon
I'll puff my cheeks,
I'll purse my lips,
I'll conjure a paper blizzard.
You'll gasp at my powers then
and call me Wizard.

Occupational Hazards

I've been cutting paper. All morning.

Not a hard task, you'd think,
a sort of moving sleep.
I might be lulled into a trance
except that one thing—
the thing I use—
has caught me up in something eerie:
the grinding noise alone dements and galls.

It's a large square tool the color of guns
but hammered out in frets, like a guitar.
Along one side, there sits a clever lever:
adamantine, bladed, cleaver-sharp.

Raise this death-piece and it lures you
with a promise of gothic shock and red:
Give me your wrist, your ring finger,
your hair, your baby's head. Give me your . . .

But I refuse to listen.
After all, it works for me. I'm the boss.

Now I'm wielding it with cool *sprezzatura.*
It's a sword and I'm a musketeer.
It's a ray gun, I am Joan of Venus:
the sheets go dropping like so many zapped foes.

When this butchering is over,
the collating begins.
I'll be sorting these for hours
over there
at the long table
where the hibernating stapler waits.

It is electric.
In use, it snaps at your hand
like a predator turtle.

Words for a Temp

There are so many risks to belonging!
You can grow fat on the sugars of conviviality
or choke on ambition's hard-edged bone
and I've known

the cloy of one, the slow suffocation
of the other. I glide through my days without
encumbrance now, a bride of detail—
no doubt—

but cool, cool. I give such small
parts of me—fingers to patter their keyboards,
a voice to trill into their phones—
and all

I get from them is something to do
and it's always quickly forgotten: a dull memo
to "word process" or a chart of numbers—
I've no clue

what they mean. How excited
they get over airy nothing!
From the desks I occupy, I observe
them pacing—

the nodding heads, the hands that pound
the tables and slash the air. On sunny days, their
dramas play in silhouette
against bare

windows, intolerably bright. It's awe-
some, to be sure, but not for me, never again for
me. I'm no one's food! A steady job
is a maw

that bolts you whole, a churning
gut that maculates the soul. I stay clean
as I pay a transient's tribute to the workaday
machine.

Words for a Latter-Day Luddite

I don't know what possessed me.
I only know I'd had it with that device
and its stubborn will.
Its imperfections held me back,
scattering my concentration,
wrecking my performance,
till I grew more and more nervous,
more and more unnerved,
and it got the best of me.

It was all so avoidable.
For months I had begged for the current model.
It will save time, I promised,
it will profit everyone!
I was told only *Be patient*
then silently dismissed.
Back at my desk
the machine would sit triumphant,
humming the old annoying monotone
and functioning worse than ever,
out of spite.

One day I swore and stamped
and yanked its frazzled wire from the wall
and small as I am,
carried the dead weight to the far window
where I pushed it, no, I hurled it through!
I was soon surrounded
and led to the authorities
who paid me severance
and let me go.

So I am as you see me now:
walled-in, wild-eyed!—an idler.
For some I am a heroine,
a rebel, a Fury, a flattener of false gods.

For others, a dotty nobody
to snicker at in anecdotes.
O let me whisper in my exile
of my since-life's round remorse!
Each day I live the loveless episode again
and still again
and even now I witness it before me,
as in slow motion:

the pulling of the cord,
the lifting of the weight,
the long and burdened strides
to the antiseptic pane—
then the crash,
the imploding-exploding glass,
and the apparatus
growing small
and smaller,
wheeling low,
and then the spattering,
the loss,
the echo.

Sanctuary

A plain place, all tile and porcelain.
Airless, with an echoing of heels.
Prone to leakage. Soiled
in spite of constant disinfecting.
Ill-lit. Paper-strewn.

But also private,
with a row of doors to dream behind,
a row of doors to slam
whenever a slam is necessary.
Near these, a row of sinks
to rinse the taint from our corporate hands.
And how useful the mirrors are,
reflecting a taut chin or a troubled brow,
guiding as we powder them to realignment.

Tears are welcome here, for men are not.
Talk is welcome here, for no one works.
Is it any wonder that we tarry here so often,
moved by needs more burning
than the ones the room is meant for?

So listen, fellows, peeping sidelong
beyond the closing door—

It isn't vanity that draws us to the mirrors
nor common urge that calls us to the stalls.
We are here because of the trials of there.
We are here for sanctuary.

I Hear America Complaining

24 hours a day our lines are open.
24 hours a day the people yawp.
I hear America complaining.

We haven't kept our promises.
We hoodwink with our premises.
Our truth is in too fine a print.
Our advertisements mislead.

And then there is our greed.

And then there is our service: never prompt;
our shoddy goods which ravel at the seams.
We have broken their dreams.

The customers have done their part.
They've paid and paid us and their money's green.
Our business has been their nemesis.

They allow no armistice.
Theirs is the good fight.
Quality! Indemnity! Apology!
We cower. They are always right.

My Demon Lover

. . . took form one day
as I was trilling into a telephone:
Good Morning!
Gijutsu Saishin North America.
May I help you?

Right there, at the front desk,
he knocked the phone from my grip
with a cloven hoof.

He sprang to the desk and hunched before me,
his yellow eyes bright as halogen.
His legs, if they were legs, enveloped me.

What rose from his scaled flesh
I took into my virgin's mouth
and then we blended into steam, one element;
no two beings could be closer.

Behind etched glass doors
in those tidy and decorous offices,
my demon lover had me
and had me
and had me.

And that is how I was taken by poetry
at the age of seventeen.
At a dull summer job,
in a slough of boredom,
I scrawled a few lines
about a make-believe demon lover
that reddened my cheeks with glee.

I tucked the poem under the blotter
on my last day of work,
leaving it for the new receptionist

23

who'd be Japanese, I supposed,
fastidious and shockable and shy,
and maybe she'd give a little gasp
and decide to keep it.

Green Man

. . . with your green twill shirt
and your green-leaf emblem,
green pail, green tools, green thumb—
when I rummage for evidence
of the humane around here,
you turn up, with your loamy hands.

How mildly you minister to the ficus, the pothos,
the potted ivy in its unsupported sprawl.
Desk to desk, you walk your stations,
crimping and pruning, probing, fluffing,
and humming, it seems, a hymn to Mother Ceres.

Now you take the pulse of my languishing fern,
watering it faithfully, misting its green hair.
I feel my own pulse slowing
as it does in languor
as it might in prayer
if I spent my days as you spend yours,
fostering the green potential of things.

Profit is what I cultivate
in this green building of hermetic glass,
grave and perpendicular,
with the perfect symmetry of the crystal
and a crystal's fine sterility.
Yet your plants thrive
in the hothouse brilliance of the place
and freshen our desiccated air.

And you, green man, with your green garb
and your green touch
and your indispensable green skills
are always welcome here.
We bean-counting bankers happily pay your bills.

The Beauty in the Bun

"You've got to be able to see the beauty
in a hamburger bun."
—*Ray Kroc, Founder, McDonald's*
~~~~~~~~~~~~~~~~~~~~~~~~~~~~~~~~

Admire its shapely elegance,
geodesic, plump,
yielding in texture,
female in line,
with a Braille of tickling seeds
along the dome.
Thumbable, ethereal.
And the palette!
Eggshell brown blending
to eggshell white.
Spare, modern:
a Bauhaus hassock
or a Warhol icon.
Ergonomic in contour,
rhythmic in proportion,
functional in form.
I have sold a billion,
I will sell a trillion.
I sell what people want.
They wait in line
the world over
to consume a joy forever.

Memorandum

Yes, I remember the manuscript.
It landed on my desk as an auk might,
with a thud and a flutter.
I pushed it away to tend to other business.
And then it went astray.

So please stop asking for it.
It is gone.
It vanished like a species.
These constant queries of yours
can't do a thing about it.

My aide keeps harping on it:
The loss! The loss!
She has clawed through the cabinets
three times
and each time it was hopeless.

So I have no answer for you.
You understand,
I am quite helpless.
A thing was once within my reach
and then it slipped away

into the zero zone around here somewhere—

time's breach.

Wail from the 29th Floor

Green building of sealed glass: who jails me here?
What crime is it that sent me to this chair?
What screen is this, which I am made to slave at?
Whose chains are these, which I drag and rave at,
hour by minute by morning by year?
If I remembered freedom, I'd hold it dear
but memory is mute behind my Zombie stare.
The cathode rays electrify my hair.

All these images are lies. No one compels
my fingers to the keys. Autistic spells
torment my nights but not my busy days.
I have a seemly job and the job pays.
I process words, but once I sought a grail!
It is my questing soul that writhes in jail.

Crying for Girls

Crying for girls! Wall Street requires girls.
Girls to type and file and fetch, girls
to tot their expenses, to see
to mail and phones and make coffee.
Job orders torrent in for girls.

We'll send you out this morning. Girls
like you are snapped up fast: nice girls
with smarts and personality.
Crying for girls

is all they do on Wall Street. Girls
are hard to come by, good ones, girls
like you. So sign right here, honey.
Those men on Wall Street are and shall be
wringing their hands for want of girls,
crying for girls.

Resignation

This, superiors,
is to offer you
my resignation.
Too many years have passed
without recompense
and without sentience
too many days,
each one vacant
as the bare vestibule
I pass through
day after hollow day
from or to
the circle of sorry labor
I inhabit
that is my habit,
my subordination.

Automaton,
I go about my work:
totting up numbers,
filling out forms,
stacking and stapling—
so efficient!—
but watching every minute
on your gray clock
loiter and drag,
loiter and drag
to the tired end of day.

And what of
those dear others
who share my circle,
whose faces match
my own encrypted face?
They are not dear.
Away from here

they live lives I can't imagine
in strange and singular worlds
that have no place for me.
If there is friendship here,
it's made of shallow stuff,
of pleasantries,
enforced equivalence:
the accident of company.

"I will seek work elsewhere!"
That has been my quest.
A foolish enterprise:
the grail's of Styrofoam at best.
Wherever I go,
I meet your duplicate:
vestibule, paperwork,
watched clocks
and gray-eyed vacancy.
What's the good of going?
I'm too weary now
to take my future in my hands
and forge another way.
This, superiors,
is to offer you my resignation.
I'll stay.

2. Practical Lies

Vices and Follies

Universe Management

In this glass tower overlooking our illimitable city,
a manager mistakes his customers for the cosmos.
I am willing to grant him this one delusion.
The numbers are staggering, after all.
Fifty million people tuck our plastic in their pockets
on this continent alone!

Now consider each customer's "uniqueness"—
how one flaunts our product for prestige
while another likes its value pricing,
another its wide acceptance and utility.
Really there are as many reasons why our product
is consumed as there are consumers,
as many reasons as there are stars in the night sky!

How to bring order to this chaos?
How to cluster these myriad souls
with their elusive motives
into sense-making constellations
so that our product may be customized to please each user
while our brand, like the sun,
remains fixed and trustworthy and true?
This is the mission of the universe manager.
Ours is named Bob. He does a yeoman's job.

Meanwhile, that other universe expands or contracts,
advertising its amoeboid galaxies
in an infinite medium of matter bright or dark,
welcoming the commerce of the comet,
the flimflam of the supernova,
and managing itself well enough.
With natural law to guide it,
it has enjoyed an unparalleled longevity.

In the glass tower
the manager doesn't think much about natural law.

It's the laws of the marketplace he quails before,
calming himself, however imperfectly,
with the anodynes of research and statistical modeling,
spending his bonuses on cars called Mercury or Saturn,
and continuing to believe, against all evidence,
that his efforts ultimately matter
in this or any universe.

The Manager of Change

So:
You want to "re-engineer" this stodgy company
and make it vigorous and nimble,
streamlined in its every process,
downsized yet outsize,
jump-started for the future,
cutting edge in the now.
You have change in mind, my friend,
radical, root-ripping change.
People will not welcome it.
Why would people welcome it?
Haven't we watched the cooing baby
mutate into the foul-mouthed teen,
the meddlesome granny
become the indifferent corpse?
Haven't we noted our own faces
morphing in the mirror,
season by season, year by year,
as our youthful hopes segued into dread
and our innocence into dry cynicism?

So:
we hate change, we fear it,
no matter how we blather in interviews
about our fitness for these shifty, shifting times.

You can't can us all and hope to prosper
so what is the solution?

Your high-priced self-employed consultant
will whip up a transition plan
containing the usual ingredients—
a measure of teamwork, a pinch of empowerment,
all of it rather over-larded with unctuous optimism.
Still there will be griping and gossip and low morale,
defiance and dawdling and resignations.

You're prepared for these little treasons.
You have faith that we will yield to all your reasons.
It is just a matter of time—

but more time than you've factored for.
What should take six months will take a year,
what should take a year will take three
at which point you will notice
(if you haven't been canned yourself)
that a whiff of obsolescence has infiltrated
your carefully crafted stratagem,
a faint, portending stink of putrefaction.

So:
you will pound your fist
on your coffin-heavy desk
and call a meeting
and call for change.

An Office Bestiary

Beware of that one.
He's a nuisance.
He insists, he insists,
his nasal noise
the luckless ear's affliction.
How he buzzes
with unnecessary news,
pursuing, pursuing,
always in front of you,
always there
when you turn around!
He's a *gnat*, we say.
He's never brushed away
for very long.

Beware of that one.
She may be poised
but what she's poised for
is savagery.
Note the toothy smirk,
the pointed nails,
the clenched and agile haunches.
When you least expect it,
she'll pounce.
In front of everyone
she'll pin you down,
she'll tear you up,
she'll chew you out.
She's a *pit bull*, we say.
She's never kept at bay
for very long.

Beware this last one
most of all.
Though he lays low,
he's high-minded.

Slick talk, flattery,
that conspiratorial grin—
he'll appeal to you,
you'll be drawn in.
Then he'll turn on you.
All you have been granted
will be lost.
Then you'll see him
for what he is,
a *snake* who stalked you,
cold-of-eye, cold-blooded,
reptilian in every way.

Reptile. Canine. Insect.
Partly human?
Ask it. Bray.

The Misbegotten Detention
of the Unkempt

It was just too harrowing, having to see them every day
in their tube tops, stretch pants, zoot suits,
wrinkled shirt-tails trailing behind them,
mole-strewn clavicles jutting ahead!
We have them in custody now.
We sent them down to sub-floor four
to have their photos taken for a new I.D.,
an entirely false premise.
Instead we locked them in a cinder block room,
having emptied it of its store of cooler water
and obsolete computer monitors.

Nothing to do now
but watch them on closed-circuit television.
Some shake their fists and grimace,
others pace, others do nothing much.
That sad sack in the moth-eaten sweater?
He doesn't bathe much, I can vouch for it.
That redhead in the mini with the orangutan gams?
She picks her zits in the cafeteria, just like she's doing now.
That sleazeball with the comb-over and the rubber thongs
rakes his toenails every chance he gets.

I confess I have a bit of a crush on Carla.
She loiters with me in the coffee room every morning;
oh, what sways inside her muumuu as she sugars and stirs!
If only she'd brushed her teeth once in a while,
I might have spared her this ignominy.

The re-educators are due at any moment.
They'll administer electric shock and refuse potty breaks.
They'll demonstrate flossing
and pass around fliers for wing tips and sensible heels.
But will they change these people?
I suspect it is vain to think so.

The fact is, they aren't like us, they aren't vain!
What we see when we look their way
doesn't interest them a whit.
Sooner or later we'll have to release them
and they'll mingle among us again,
smelly, unkempt, oblivious, innocent, free.

Presence of the Absence

You phoned it in.
You called in out.
Just a little "mental health day";
who could fault it?
An a.m. on the couch, crocheting,
and in the p.m. a meander and a browse.
You didn't realize that your absence
would be so closely noted.

One came by for a copy of your cheat sheet
and left empty-handed.
One reached deep inside your drawers.
One umbilicaled his laptop to your *brother*
and printed an entire presentation.
And that stern one from Compliance:
how she lingered at your empty chair,
arms folded, scowling and cooling her heels!
It's all going on your permanent record.
The evidence is plain.
On every cellcam, webcam, digicam,
there you are not.

Practical Lies

A vibrant woman at the apex of her powers
tells me *sotto voce* that she lies.
She's masked a black eye with white makeup.
On the day of her abortion
she called in sick with backache.
Men "get" backache; she works with many men.

I too must fashion a lie, she advises,
in the name of self-worth and good reputation.
"Tell them you took time off
to care for a dying aunt," she says.
"Tell them it wasn't possible to call,
tell them she needed you every minute."
I practice speaking the practical lie.
I tell it to a mirror till I'm quite convincing.

I tell it to you now.
My aunt was very ill.
I fed her with a spoon and slept in her hospital room
and wrangled with doctors.
Then I buried her.
I'm so sorry that I missed a month's work
but I'm back now,
ready to prevaricate, ready to go on.

Morning in Sodom

. . . and the fog is lifting. A chancre-sun
reddens at the lip of haze. As I weave
through a warp of pushing bodies, I cleave
my mind to last night's carnal exhibition
I had tried to scour into sink and drain.
Let me rush to cool offices of commerce
where the flesh is quashed, where only the purse
opens in greed! But I go against the grain.

Buildings slant, there's racket, smoke is looming:
I step in a sinister promenade.
Beneath crisp suits, behind designer frames,
I sense an animality that grooming
shields only from the pure. These walkers claim
an eminence they do not own. I know that masquerade.

Travailelle

We work with spite or rue.
We earn a bit, a lot.
We drown in what we do.

Outside a cosmic view
dwarfs us to a dot:
we haven't got a clue.

We dare not look. A few
may look. So few. So what?
We drown in what we do.

The holy sages knew
that getting's a garrote.
We haven't got a clue.

We get and spend and woo.
We want: a dhow, a yacht.
We drown in what we do.

Is there a path more true
to some more ample spot?
We haven't got a clue.
We drown in what we do.

3. Love and Work

Getting It Done

... meant late hours at vast tables,
the moon in duplicate in shining wood.
It meant meetings at dawn,
luminous dawn,
orange fire lashing the majestic panes.
O Agni of the seven tongues! O radiance.
How could we fail, washed by that light?

How could we not be kind?
I brought you coffee,
you rubbed my shoulders,
Manny broke the tension with his silly jokes.
We had a job to do, together, and we did it—
we who lack the selflessness of the hive mind.

We'll be rubbing our own shoulders soon,
back in our separate cubes,
and mapping out new paths for our own careers.
But for now, let's exult
for we got it done,
we are undivided,
many and one.

After Long Days Visiting the Nursing Home, I Return to the Office

... to screen calls,
take minutes,
tweak numbers,
draft, deal, fax,
fix coffee,
smile the robotic smile.

How well everyone seems,
gesticulating forcefully,
walking unfalteringly on sound legs.
No one says *fork* when he means *briefcase*,
no one snores at the conference table
or slumps limply at her desk, dribbling.
Our chairs have wheels
but only so we can work faster,
swiveling deftly in the direction of vital purposes.

Odd, then, that breezing by a certain open door,
I catch sight of Manny, in his shirtsleeves,
motionless, emotionless, corpse-eyed,
no purpose in his eyes at all.
I hurry by
but sidewise I perceive his silhouette,
faint behind a scored glass wall.
His head is in his hands now,
his spine bows,
his weary posture an augury of times to come.

The Blood Drive

It wasn't altruism—
that inconclusive, random love—
nor force, nor civic pride
that brought me here.
I gave blood selfishly,
for the feel of my own blood
sliding away from me.
For the thrill.

For surely, I thought, it must be thrilling
to shut your eyes in limp surrender
and sit up moments later changed,
lightheaded, lightened, newly pure.
Such a practice was for an epoch the universal cure!
Remembering that, and all the great
who were bled before me,
I was greedier than ever for the ceremony,
the pomp under the bright red cross.

O I admit it—
I enjoy these violent speculations
and have yoked the most vagrant happenstances
to an ox of serendipity and high design.
And it works.
My contortions uplift the commonest episodes
for a time.

But this time
it seems my wits fail me
for there is no glamor
in the jab of the clinical needle,
the pulse of the literal blood,
and I lie on the table
not as poet or martyr
but as I am—
a skin-bound being

living on the earth,
watching, wincing
as a strange red piping
thrums from my pale arm, umbilical—
and I am no one, and anyone:
drawn vessel,
time's vassal,
hammering heart.

At last I rise and walk,
diminished
yet relieved—
at ease now
in the company of other donors.
They have given each of us a badge.
And as we leave,
scattering to our assorted offices,
I am stricken by a most unexpected ardor,
without focus, without margin,
claiming nothing,
making no sense at all
yet it lifts me up—
an inconclusive,
utterly random,
utterly restful love.

Waiting for Elevation

"We are living now in an age of inventions, and we no longer have to
take the trouble of climbing stairs for . . . the elevator has replaced these
very successfully . . . I desire an elevator to raise me to Jesus."
—*Ste. Thérèse de Lisieux*

~~~~~~~~~~~~~~~~~~~~~~~~~~~~~~~~~~~~

This typical morning
as I loiter
with a gang of coworkers
laden with papers
and dribbly take-out coffee,
I too desire an elevator.
Let it lift me
to my cluttered cube,
where I'll hunker down,
efface in work,
succumb to menial offices—
as you, Thérèse,
were once subsumed by yours.
At last a green light,
a chime:
we throng into
a mirrored cell
and are raised,
Little Flower,
to a more lofty station
than you ever
could have prophesied.
There, beyond glass,
the sacred spire;
there the bridges,
the helicopter,
the skyscraper,
and all the radiant logos
of our global souk!
It is indeed

a dazzling vantage—
but Saint, in your mercy,
raise us higher still.
As we do and are done to,
in the crucible
of our humdrum jobs,
give us holiness.
Grant us ecstasy
even in dailiness.

Women Dancing With Women

Another corporate shindig:

Let the men in right
ties who might
twirl with us

stay tight
in gray groups,
rigid in their might—

we'll shimmy under strobes
without them! Light

on our feet,
liquid in our hips,
we make a snazzy company

O we're a sight—
strutting and bumping
twisting, pumping,

ecstatic in our machinations,
black, white—
a moving patchwork quilt

of silk and spandex
snapping on its line

and from that height

we raise our jeweled arms
and shout out
quavering syllables—
each of us a star in Vegas,
each a sprite

among sprights

and now pinstriped scarecrows
turn bald heads
toward the happy rite
we're conjuring
this minute and that minute

and all the witchy night!

Dead Matter

Buried under the manuscript, cut
pages of text,
her author's verbal glut—

off-topic, prolix.
The quick fix?
Kill the extraneous, put it to rest.

He's shocked at first. So much effort
wasted! "Must we abort
this bit or that bit

just because it's imperfect?
Is there no way to deflect
your pitiless verdict?"

Though she's been a second mom
to him, now she's *la belle dame
sans merci.*

Eventually, he accepts the fate
of the killed pages. They weren't great,
he grants,

they didn't merit being read.
They are better off dead.
When the book is published—

dazzling jacket, author photo, heft—
he's no longer bereft.
He forgets the dead matter.

She does not. The disquieting ghost
of her expurgations haunts her
every night—

so many passages done away
with, wiped away,
so many words lost forever.

She was the only one
who read them at all, she is their lone
griever.

Corporate Retreat

The planning team
for MagnaCard's department of credit marketing
went rafting on the Sidewinder River.

The mission?
Revitalize the team
and rev up for another year's objectives!

Together in our borrowed wetsuits
we took our places in the rubber raft,
we negotiated rapids.

There was slow water too,
so unlike the churning engine back at M-Card
you couldn't draw a parallel.

Osprey lighted in aeries on the banks
or spiraled upward, grazing the high cliffs.

Manny slipped into the river for an impromptu swim.
We watched him drift beside us,
borne along by the same current.
Usually he's a big talker
but all he said was, "It's good."

That's when I was lost to myself.
I wasn't from the city anymore
but from some forfeited, imperishable place
beneath venture, beyond thought,
where there were no boundaries,
no skin at all between the principalities.

Then, horseplay:
someone threw water on me from a full bucket.
My sunglasses dripped; where was clarity?
I shook my head like a drenched mutt

and smiled the necessary smile.

The next run of rapids soaked everyone.
On each of our desks you'll find a photo,
stopping those rapids in time
and also Manny, back on board and whooping,
and a dozen others, paddling as one,
and me too, wide awake
and surging along with the others.

Off Duty

I won't go into detail.
That would be talking shop.
I will say only:
I have made many promises.
Some are set down in contracts.
Others go unworded
but they bind me just the same—
in the breath, in the blood,
wherever ambition burns
and invention blossoms.
I am sworn.
I have made promises.
And when I have kept today's,
tomorrow's will want keeping
and the next week's, next year's
and even my dreams
are full of press and clutter
and when I wake from them
I wake late and headachy
and I have to get going,
I haven't a moment to spare.

All the same
a moment is what I did spare.
Just this morning
at the kitchen window
I took a breath
that nourished no ambition,
furthered no lofty need.
It met no deadline,
paid no outstanding bill.
It was time stolen, time won.
There was simply no accounting for it!

Certainly I had meant no pilferage.
I was simply drinking coffee,

a stoic's drink, and fuel for the engine too.
And my brain was fully occupied
with lists and schedules,
tasks of every kind.

But then I felt it:
the great hearth warmth.
Earth's own healer sun was beaming in on me.
Clear through my sweater,
clear through my scrubbed skin
the heat bored.
And I wondered:
when had the season shifted?
How had the planet wheeled so near her star
without my taking note of it?
I touched my spoon.
The chrome was burning!
I closed my eyes.
The hubbub in my brain went mute.

My moment passed and I was out the door,
fluffing my hair and flailing for a cab.
I had made a nine o'clock promise.
I was already unconscionably late.

Torpid Transit

On the E Train a woman yawns
and then a woman yawns
and yawns spawn around the crowded car
and many mouths dilate, many lungs swell.

I yawn myself
and gawk into another open throat, uvula waving.

I yawn again
and watch as heads slump forward
in a heedless doze.

A druggie sleeps on his feet right next to me.
One hand, aloft, grabs on to only air.
He tilts and sways in the harness of his trance
and is held; he does not fall.

At 53rd and Lex, I summon an atom of vim
and exit the car with others like me,
hundreds of other people,
merging in procession, going off to work.

Two by two, on a machinery of looping steps,
we ascend, very slowly,
out of the underworld, into the upperworld,
toward the arousing light.

Our deadpan eyes roll up in that direction.
We fill ourselves with one last Lethe-gulping yawn.

Invitation to a Baby Shower
in the Corporate Law Library

Noreen's day is near. Please join us.
Along leather volumes, brown and black,
we have strung the pastel crêpe.
On the mahogany table: strawberry shortcake,
pink punch, blue grapes, green tea.
Come. Partake.
Join us at the dark table, and revere.

Join us at the dark altar. We'll speak of birthing.
By the leather tomes, with their sterile codes,
we will stake our fertile claim.
Noreen will sit and stroke her ample belly.
We'll plate for her, and you, a wealth of cake.

She will open bibs and rattles, an eyelet blanket.
She will mention the show of blood and the helping gash.
The mothers among us will tell of our various labors.
The childless among us will listen with worshipful awe.
Come worship.

Abandon your desk for an hour. Observe an advent.
Heed a profound and uncodified corporate law.
In this sober place: cake and high laughter,
women, a woman, a mystery, offerings, tales.

Fifth Avenue Gothic

What hath befallen me? Ah, I have been hurled
headlong to another building, and a low and lowly floor,
no more
to glimpse the gauzy fogs furled

along the girders of the Queensborough Bridge,
no more to watch reflected sunsets
blazing from steel ridge to steel ridge.
Even an army Quonset

hut hath more charm than this ill-lit
cubicle with surfaces
of gray eye-aching Formica. Worse still: writ
large on this building is the address

of this building, triple sixes, 666,
the apocalyptic number of the beast.
Forsooth, evil tricks
have been visited upon me here, my least

request for a working phone
or a zone
for mail hath proved a grim
futility. Lights flare then flicker then dim.

There is one window and one window
only which I may, at isolated moments, rest
before. If I crane, a small street-show
edges into sight—clotted taxis, the manifold urban mess.

What I see mostly, what fills my limited vision,
is Saint Thomas Episcopal
Church, or anyway a portion
of it, a fragment of one intricate stone wall.

Holiness, however small! The granite saints

in niches gaze mildly and hold fast
and seem to bless the taints
and derelictions cooked up in these vast

financial corridors across the way.
The Gothic cinquefoils catch a morning ray
but the larger clerestory windows keep very dark.
Each day they bear the mark

of 666, its pitiless adumbration,
and I bear it too,
who dwelleth where the shadow emanates, who
lifteth yet her arms in yearning adoration

of those sculpted saints and of that architecture
and Christ too, Logos and Love's avatar,
lodged, some say, within that church's tabernacle,
and in my heart as well, no matter the obstacle—

despair, ambition, ire, greed, idolatry.
From the heavens to the abyss
the seraphs proclaim His mercy, and so let me
though I desperately wave from the devil's own edifice.

The Triumph of Eros

In a bull market, a depression grips us.
We shamble to meetings with drooping heads,
we wear a plain and shapeless garb.

We are like monks, practicing custody of the eyes;
like nuns, shunning "particular" friendship.
Eros must be vanquished for the common good.
It says so, right here in the employee manual.

Perhaps Peg and Don haven't read it
for I spied them today, necking in the copy room.
Peg will soon be fired, if past experience repeats,
or one will be sent to Brussels, the other to Albuquerque.
One way or another, the situation will be "handled."

I worked once in an old loft building, plagued by mice.
We kept cats around to hunt them—
two neutered tabbies, fat, snoozy,
more unsexed than the drabbest of company drones.
Yet I came upon them one day, coupling on my boss's desk,
rumbling and yowling in feline transport,
shedding all over his blotter and lawyerly files.
I shut the door and left them to their shameless offices.

A Roadblock in the Negotiations

When it happens, it happens after hours.
Discord in our midst. Baring of claws.
What have we done to raise daemonic powers?

Undone, a good day's work! What devours
the crumbs we threw, concessions to the cause?
When it happens, it happens after hours.

Fatigued, we clash with bitter words and glowers,
in thrall, it seems, to elemental laws.
What have we done to raise daemonic powers?

Why not settle? Must we clutch what's "ours"?
A matter of fate, perhaps, of human flaws?
When it happens, it happens after hours

as patience flags and interdependence sours.
This force discomfits even as it awes.
What have we done to raise daemonic powers?

So we are stuck and slump like wilted flowers.
Agreement nears then teases then withdraws.
When it happens, it happens after hours.
What have we done to raise daemonic powers?

Quotidian Ballad

The man-in-the-corner-office's wife is dying.
His clothes after lunch have an ethery hospital smell.
Whenever he says "Good morning," we know he's lying.
Whenever we say "Good morning," he knows we're lying.

He's still our boss, although we've caught him crying.
We do our jobs under robotic spell.
We'd like to help but solace seems like prying.
His armored bearing: shield against all prying.

They say she's near the end: rumors are flying.
He's late a lot, he always looks like hell.
From out of the conference room sails a professional sighing.
Into the phones, over the networks: sighing.

Pleasantries no longer work. There's no belying:
in every ear there gongs a galling bell.
The man-in-the-corner-office's wife is dying.
The man-in-the-corner-office's wife is dying.

High Floor Ballad

Raise the shades, let fog reveal us
    even as it blinds.
Shut the lights off. Turn the phones off.
    Hush your chattering minds.
    Hush your chattering minds.

Stand before these opaque windows
    Something may be seen.
Press your cheek to the delicate glass.
    Press your palm there. Lean.
    Palm there. Press there. Lean.

Gaze into uncanny dimness.
    Gaze into the gray.
Within the cloud, unknowing blurs
    into a clarity.
    Into a clarity.

Raise the blinds and take the cloud in,
    breathe the absolving haze.
Let it inform us, let it suffuse us.
    These are the lucid days.
    Breathe the absolving haze.

Love and Work

They say it all comes down to love and work.
Our lot: incessant dance of love and work.

We build, we serve, we cling, we yield,
we give, we're given over: love and work.

The dance exhausts. We're strained and pulled apart,
injured and used up by love and work.

The dance elates, arouses, lifts us high.
We're spry. We strike a balance: love and work.

Or if we trip we still go reeling on.
Jobless, lacking mate, we love and work.

But does it all come down to love and work?
The lilies of the field don't love or work

and yet, O Lord, it's said you tend them well,
who merely are, who do not love or work.

4. After

Canticle from a Cubicle

God, how stupidly I spend my time
on work I don't like
with people who see me as cold-blooded and gruff.
If it were money I was spending
I'd own tchotchkes, trinkets, useless stuff.

At my post at work, I've set down amulets:
a statue of triumphant Nike,
a print of the Bayeux tapestry—
but Victory is small in this outfit
and the Norman Conquest doesn't fit my cubicle.
I've lopped off half the chronicle.

My computer speaks; I've programmed it thus:
In the a.m.. it says *Hello, gorgeous.*
In the p.m. *You'll be back.*
Next a.m. I am. I'm no slack.
I can be counted on, I am reliable,
I'm what they want here, "proactive" yet pliable.

God, how did it come to this at all?
This is not, this never has been, my call.
Am I just an addict, perhaps, hooked on the rut,
beholden to the machinery, hot for the money?
Or a clown, a lady Pagliacci, butt
of all jokes, pretending this tragedy is funny?

I don't know. I know not one sure thing.
My hope is on hold and yet I hope to hope.
I am better off here for a while. Nope.
I am better off out. Nike, lend me a wing,
lead me away, let me rise up and quit!
Deliver me now from the keyboard and desk where I sit.

Let Go

Enough of your allegations and ill will!
You are not the only one whose job was discontinued.
In every directorate there were insufficiencies
and before the re-org,
wasteful redundancies across the board.
Headhunters brought in new blood.
Can you fault us for going forward?

Year to year, you could wander from floor to floor
and still not locate your corner office!
We took the walls down,
we set up modules, supple spaces.
Even the desks have wheels.
Flexibility is the core skill these days
and you were never made of pliant clay.
Fired to the breaking point is what you were,
shards are what you've become.
You are not useful to anyone anymore.

After

You were sure you'd packed everything—
family photographs, your Steuben paperweight,
that extra pair of shoes—
yet you rummage through the deep carton,
clawing at tissue, popping bubble wrap.
Something is amiss and something's missing.

Here's the company phone book and there your name in it.
Here's the silk scarf that was your parting gift.
Did they really picture you in lavender and white?
Pastel is what you are to them now,
and them to you, a watercolor viewed at a distance
through memory's filmy eye.

Already you forget the name of the mail clerk,
and the access codes, and what it was, exactly,
that made this severance seem shrewd.

You had thought you were paying attention!—
but you were dreaming.
The place was a virtual reality,
absorbing, beautiful even, but strange,
the skyline views both vivid and vertiginous,
the corridors labyrinthine.
You flew down them as if in free fall.
What was the urgency?
What have you lost?
What will you do with this dusty stuff?

The Unemployment Office

I appear there every Tuesday
at the appointed time
to perform a certain ritual, a mime.

Papers change hands,
hands avow their week
of idleness. I am meek

and put my name to everything they proffer
and thus am allocated pittance
from an unseen coffer.

Other days are even stranger.
Without routine to anchor the floating hours,
morning's a danger,

afternoon a nullity in space.
Attempting nothing, the self is mortified.
There is no saving face.

Meals are waited for like kisses.
Mail is counted on like sons.
Mind broods on the body's excretions.

There's flow and enterprise outside
but clutter shuts me in—
I 'm maid of the vacuum, Mussbed's bride,

laundress of tatters, mother of snags
as sheets are shook by washers
then cooked into knotted rags.

And so it goes. One eye
is fixed on clock and calendar,
day out, day in. Somehow I get by—

Tuesday comes. I have a purpose then,
a place in line, the solace
of the automatic rite, less

than sacrament and more. All around,
agents of this civil service
minister their dole. They pound

the date on everything they touch—
so fond of exactitude!
I am in their clutch.

Even when I've left, their malediction
hovers like an aura
and I am classified: not fauna, not flora

but an utterly useless being
in an utterly isolate niche.
Far off beyond seeing

there may be an end, of course. A start.
But for now I must tend to this corner
of Void. It is my part.

In Company

After two years of writhing solitude
I come back to the crude
arena of the living, to take my place
at a front desk, recast my face
and welcome callers to a fabric
company. Nearby, my pick
of seven beds, each arranged
with the firm's designs: deranged
ferns, bulbous roses,
cats, dogs, in supplicant poses.
On sleazy 32nd Street we show our wares.
In the back room, six artists share
four drawing boards and are forever
quarreling. Allegiances sever,
complaints are croaked into the tainted
air. And still the hideous patterns are painted.

When the chairman has a heart attack
and the glamorous design chief gets the sack
and the artists finally blacken
one another's eyes, I do not slacken
off as once I might have. Instead
I am alert to chime and phone, wed
to the work as a honeymooning bride
is wed to untiring ecstasy. O I tried
the way of the anchorite and became
no purer than I'm becoming in this game
of argument and hustle and stale woes!
If my calling be to hawk the garish rose
then I accept my calling. To be
imperfect and of use is all I ask: to be

    in company.

Coda

The Transformation

The Transformation

We couldn't say when it started exactly, the transformation.
Interoffice envelopes began arriving with our names
in fine calligraphy: that was an initial sign.
Then a young manager gave a presentation
using words like *gouache* and *crescendo*
and the bullet points on his overheads
were like icons from the Book of Kells.
Soon after, we stopped ordering deli platters
wrapped in cellophane, favoring
delicate quiches instead, or an array of soups,
or sushi delivered by a tranquil gent
who set our conference table with a studied reverence.
Our divisional vice president cultivates orchids now,
our receptionist displays pots and pots of African violets.
We set aside days for cultural celebration
when the office is a panoply of turbans and kimonos,
kilts, saris, dirndls and dashikis.
Other days we wear an item of like color, or white.
Sometimes a hush settles over the crowded cafeteria,
the cacophony dissolving into a great silence.
And just this morning, our companionable computers
booted up with the tinkling of Zen bells.
A message materialized on every screen:
We have gathered here today
to engage in joyful livelihood.
Let it engage us entirely,
that we may be enlightened and fulfilled.

About the Author

Kate Bernadette Benedict is the author of the poetry collection *Here from Away* (CW Books, 2003) and the editor of three online journals: *Umbrella: A Journal of Poetry and Kindred Prose*, *Bumbershoot* (*Umbrella*'s lighter offshoot), and *Tilt-a-Whirl*, a "sporadical" of repeating-form poetry.

Her poems have been appearing in literary journals since 1980, and she has also contributed to many anthologies, most recently *Beyond Forgetting: Poetry and Prose About Alzheimer's Disease; Not A Muse: A World Poetry Anthology; Letters to the World: Poems from the Wompo Listserv; Able Muse Anthology;* and *Hot Sonnets.*

Kate lives in New York City where she has held positions both temporary and permanent at more than one hundred corporations and nonprofits. These jobs ranged from one day in length, as with a certain philanthropy, to three years at a renowned book publisher, to fourteen years in the credit card department of a major financial institution. Inspired by these experiences, *In Company* includes poems written over three decades.

CPSIA information can be obtained at www.ICGtesting.com
Printed in the USA
BVOW072309301211

279543BV00001B/10/P